TAROT

AN ILLUSTRATED JOURNAL

by Dennis Fairchild
Illustrations by Julie Paschkis

RUNNING PRESS
PHILADELPHIA · LONDON

© 1996, 2002 by Running Press
Illustrations © 1996, 2002 by Julie Paschkis
All rights reserved under the Pan-American
and International Copyright Conventions

Printed in China

9   8   7   6   5   4   3   2
Digit on the right indicates the number of this printing

ISBN 0-7624-1354-9

Cover by Julie Paschkis
Interior design by Serrin Bodmer
Edited by Melissa Wagner
Typography: Granjon and Greco-Deco

This book may be ordered by mail from the publisher.
Please include $2.50 for postage and handling.
But try your bookstore first!

Running Press Book Publishers
125 South Twenty-second Street
Philadelphia, Pennsylvania 19103-4399

Visit us on the web!
www.runningpress.com

TAROT

THE ORIGIN OF THE TAROT is one of history's unsolved mysteries. Forecasting probably began with the elderly—those who had lived long enough to learn that everything in life changes in cycles. The seasons come and go, the wind's direction swings from north to east, the constellations move through the sky, there are births and burials, plantings and harvests.

By observing the cyclical nature of life, the older generations knew that all setbacks or failures were temporary. They encouraged their children and grandchildren with wise words like "Everything changes with time." From there, it was just a small step to realizing that life cycles could be charted and correlated to more concrete, observable patterns. Stars could be watched, calendars consulted, cards read.

The seventy-eight cards of the Tarot make up one of the tools of encouragement and empowerment that have emerged throughout the centuries. Cards 0 through 21 are known as the Major Arcana. (*Arcana* means "profound secrets" or "mysteries.") The rest of the deck consists of the four suits of the Minor Arcana: Cups, Pentacles, Swords, and Wands.

THE MAJOR ARCANA

The Major Arcana cards represent major lessons to be mastered on the road of life. These cards symbolize the range of human life—physical, intellectual, emotional, and spiritual. Explore your strengths and weaknesses, hopes and fears—the deepest part of your personality.

ZERO · THE FOOL

 Take things as they are. Matters are proceeding as planned. Do your part to settle outstanding disagreements. Kill others with kindness and let them suffer the consequences of their actions. This is a good time to build your investments or remodel your home.

When reversed: Schedules are full, time is at a premium. Take time to enjoy life's pleasures. Postpone business decisions temporarily. Use discretion and patience.

I · THE MAGICIAN

 Do you feel the adrenaline rushing through your veins? Now is the time to stretch yourself and test your limits. Be adventurous, daring, and competitive—within limits. Success and recognition will follow. It's an excellent time to begin new projects.

When reversed: Pay attention to rules and think twice before acting. Don't close yourself off from the help and guidance of others. Beware of arrogance. Make friends, not enemies.

II · THE HIGH PRIESTESS

Trust your intuition more than your reason; act more on feelings than on facts. Take your time to think about your options. Tackle difficulties with enthusiasm— these are opportunities to learn. To be a winner now, don't withdraw.

When reversed: You're expecting things to come too easily. Be careful not to give up right away when they don't. You're feeling a desire to escape, to withdraw into yourself. Shrug off your current lack of focus and work diligently to achieve your goals.

III · THE EMPRESS

Express your ideas and take calculated risks. Getting what you want is your responsibility. Your passions are of primary importance to you now. News of a wedding, pregnancy, or children arrives.

When reversed: Are you feeling inferior about your intellect, education, or communication skills? Stop it! Don't exaggerate your fears or be reluctant to take action. Problems with your mother and other intimate women are imminent.

IV · THE EMPEROR

Play by the rules and don't take shortcuts. Use common sense when managing your resources. Now is the time to get organized and make plans. Careful use of logic and reason will deliver success.

When reversed: Despite your obvious talents, success comes slowly at this time. Respect the past and learn from it. Frustrations, obstacles, delays, or setbacks will test your perseverance. Don't react too hastily; make sure all your decisions are unemotional. Balance work with play.

V · THE HIEROPHANT

 Follow the path that is familiar. Now is a good time to show how conventional you can be. Your public image and status with friends or in the community are of great concern to you now. Don't sacrifice your beliefs or freedoms for status. Keep alert to the outside world.

When reversed: Make things happen by taking care of details. Don't become too rigidly attached to order and routine—the ritual shouldn't mean more to you than the result. Personal growth comes through modesty and compassion.

VI · THE LOVERS

Lovers and close friends take center stage. Take the time to tell those closest to you what they mean to you. Examine all of your relationships that are going nowhere—eliminate the unwanted and unnecessary.

When reversed: Exaggeration abounds, emotions run high—especially jealousy. Beware of self-indulgence and greed. Slow down. Don't let anyone rush you or push you into things.

VII · THE CHARIOT

Victories are on your horizon. Reject negative people but don't judge them harshly. Appeal to others' sense of fair play. This is a very good time for travel, taking a break, and getting away.

When reversed: People are more defensive now. Don't give in to intimidation or pressure. No one wants to waste time. Expect last-minute cancellations of plans.

VIII · JUSTICE

What goes around comes around. Seek legal counsel, ask advice from elders. You may be embroiled in negotiations or tedious bureaucratic systems. Do healthy things—spiritually and physically.

When reversed: Tell the truth or get ready to suffer the consequences. Your friends are wishy-washy now. Do your part to say what's real, what's right, and what you feel. Let go of the past and resolve to turn over a new leaf.

IX · THE HERMIT

Break an unnecessary habit. Take steps to eliminate unhealthy ruts and routines. Have some of your "friends" been driving you crazy? Now is a good time to get them out of your life. Don't let yourself get stuck in the expectations of others.

When reversed: Spend time with someone you love; take care of unfinished business. Don't let your responsibilities weigh you down and stay away from anything that goes against your grain.

X · THE WHEEL OF FORTUNE

You made your bed, now you must lie in it. Own up to your actions and responsibilities—or suffer the consequences. Be true to yourself. Try something new.

When reversed: Luck isn't on your side just now. Don't get embroiled in anything you'll regret—stay constructively selfish. This is not a good time to be alone, though. Ask questions, seek answers, try options.

XI · STRENGTH

Love conquers all. Avoid pettiness and prejudice. Try to be a peace maker. Weigh all sides of every situation. Don't be so set in your ways that you miss the big picture by focusing on details. Stubbornness is your challenge of the moment.

When reversed: Everyone expects the best from you and vice-versa. Arguments with your lover or close associates are likely now. Don't give in to intimidation or pressure, and never go to bed angry. Are you seeing things realistically? Wait one more day to take action.

XII · THE HANGED MAN

Rise above material concerns and the way things have always been. Try another avenue. Relax and rethink. Keep everything aboveboard. Allow others to change their minds and look at new options. Contemplate, don't agitate.

When reversed: Stop being so close-minded. There are plenty of alternatives and solutions to your problems. Try something new. This is no time to be lazy or melancholy.

XIII · DEATH

You are entering a growing phase. Acknowledgment comes slowly. No one will offer a helping hand unless you beg for it. Don't take "no" as a final answer. Avoid self-pity. Get rid of some old habits. Stop doing anything that doesn't feel right for you.

When reversed: This card suggests you are egocentric. Be prepared to lend a shoulder and a handkerchief. Ask for a favor—and offer one, too. Setbacks and delays are likely. This is a great time for healthy escapism. Honesty brings rewards.

XIV · TEMPERANCE

 Compromise brings happiness. Perhaps you're not viewing matters objectively? Try to see the other side of the story. Use common sense and good management. The people around you are more set in their ways now. Postpone arguments and debates until they can open their minds.

When reversed: Those around you are playing to win. Don't be foolish or self-centered, but don't believe all you hear, either. There's lots of posturing in the air. Accept favors and be kind, but always listen to your higher self.

XV · THE DEVIL

Matter overpowers mind. Desires rule. Beware of your dark side. The pursuit of materialistic or sensual pleasures may taint your ability to think clearly. Cleanse yourself of behaviors and habits that are doing you no good.

When reversed: Things are unclear for you now. Don't let yourself be intimidated and don't judge others too harshly. Others seem uptight, set in their ways. Are you? Don't let past issues cloud today's progress.

XVI · THE TOWER

Everyone wants to be admired. Others embellish the truth, but what's necessary and real will prevail. Illusions will be shattered, enemies revealed. Don't be upset if things don't turn out as planned. Try to compromise and see others' points of view.

When reversed: Delays are inevitable. A fall from glory is likely. Be prepared to change course midstream. Cooperation is minimal; pushiness is plentiful. Meet opposition with compassion and sympathy.

XVII · THE STAR

 This is the card of optimism and hope. You have a chance to start over in long-standing situations. Beware of pride; aim for cooperation and innovation.

When reversed: Remain humble. You'll need imagination to come up with options for action now. Examine and evaluate issues carefully.

XVIII · THE MOON

People are acting clannish and very emotional. Don't join the crowd. Read between the lines. Your intuition is very strong right now, but you're still likely to be deceived. This is not the time to start anything new. Have patience.

When reversed: Everyone wants things done his or her way, so go easy on yourself. Take a mental-health day to get away from your responsibilities. When you come back, roll with the punches. Don't be too trusting or willing to go the extra mile—unless you can afford it.

XIX · THE SUN

Any personal growth you achieve now will be linked to self-expression. Say what you feel when you feel it. Accept criticism and admit mistakes. Enthusiasm and self-assurance bring results. A promotion is on the horizon.

When reversed: Relationship hassles are likely. Don't get wrapped up in yourself so tightly that you ignore your partner's or others' needs. Stop being overly dramatic. Set goals realistically and try to do what's good for all parties involved.

XX · JUDGMENT

A job well done delivers many rewards; laziness is punished. Make peace—don't nit-pick yourself or others too harshly. Patience brings success. Don't be cruel. Health improves, but it may take some effort on your part.

When reversed: Your desire to escape is strong. Keep your ears open and your mouth closed. Listen. Read all the fine print. Self-esteem is low and needs a boost. Act now without fear—shift into high gear!

XXI· THE WORLD

 Look at both sides of every situation and surround yourself with those who truly love you. Refuse to get shaken when others try to undermine your confidence in your strengths and abilities. Rewards and pay-backs are just around the corner. Don't give up anything for anyone.

When reversed: Don't be too trusting. Put your faith in Number One! Pamper yourself and the object of your affection. Seek intimacy and personal happiness in all you do. Resolutions come slowly but will be worthwhile when they arrive.

THE SUIT OF CUPS

Cups are concerned with love and emotions. This suit speaks of relationships with others and of the unconscious. Upright cards reveal that your feelings are extremely sensitive—easily aroused and easily hurt. Reversed cards warn against being too detached, cool, and callous.

PAGE OF CUPS

 Don't get upset if things aren't going as you hoped. Be open to alternatives and prepare for a change of plans. Think before reacting, beware of childish behavior.

When reversed: Now is the time to be independent. Friends and coworkers may not understand your feelings. Don't let emotions overpower you and don't judge others too harshly. Patience wins in the end.

KNIGHT OF CUPS

 A break from responsibilities soon arrives. Let others pamper you. Do something nice for yourself.

When reversed: Don't be in a hurry to get things done. Stop and think things through before acting. Take a vacation and stay away from responsibilities. There is life beyond work.

QUEEN OF CUPS

Remember that life is about more than your day-to-day job and worries. Take time to examine spiritual beliefs. Don't get bogged down by trivial details or the demands of others.

When reversed: Those around you are acting stuffier than normal. Pay no attention. Take time to rethink matters, especially your eating habits.

KING OF CUPS

 Go easy on yourself and accept what the day brings. Control your temper; don't take criticism personally. Try not to feel pressured by deadlines.

When reversed: Associates seem to be plodding along very slowly. Keep a backup plan handy in case they can't keep up. Exaggeration is in the stars, so read between the lines. Find a helping hand in old friends and family.

ACE OF CUPS

 Happiness arrives soon, but it may take some effort on your part to bring it to fruition. Those around you are more emotional than usual. Don't rely on them to be the voice of reason. Postpone debates. Examine home and family issues. This is a good time to consider relocating.

When reversed: Accept assistance from others. Don't be too full of yourself. Act with determination. Know when to say no.

II OF CUPS

This is a good time to make peace with anyone who recently did you wrong. Expect a happy surprise, such as a love letter or a new relationship. Don't buy into social pressure.

When reversed: Don't be insensitive. Keep things light! Now is the time to make any outstanding apologies. Don't let anyone or anything else raise your blood pressure. People may be asking too much of you now. Find constructive ways to relieve tension.

III OF CUPS

People around you are seeking acknowledgment in the form of positive strokes or physical affection. Flexibility and adaptability will bring luck. Family problems will soon mellow.

When reversed: Don't let disappointments get in the way of your happiness. Beware of overindulgence and depression. Jealousy clouds reason.

IV OF CUPS

Take a step back and look at matters from a different perspective. You might notice that your heart has been ruling your head. Share your thoughts—don't be selfish. Do your part to settle disagreements.

When reversed: Don't jump the gun or get angry when others disagree. Political power plays are on the rise. Hurt feelings could steer you down the wrong path. Be open to new friendships and relationships.

V OF CUPS

Things are not what they seem. Keep your emotions in check. Beware of deception and illusion. Reinforce your beliefs with facts and demand the same of others. Take care of unfinished business.

When reversed: Don't let yourself be overburdened by chores and responsibilities. Rise above petty politics. Friends bring support, but it might also help to take a vacation and get away from the daily grind.

VI OF CUPS

Your personal magnetism is on the rise. Be firm in affairs of the heart. Don't let the past detract from the present. This is an excellent time to start a new love affair, renew vows, or relocate.

When reversed: Make good on all your promises but don't give in to unreasonable demands from others. Be constructive in your efforts to solve problems; refrain from being pushy. Find time for deep belly laughs and new friends.

VII OF CUPS

Truth is soon revealed. Act kindly and calmly. This is no time to lose your cool. Reevaluate matters and set some long-laid plans in motion. Call an old lover just to say you're a better person for having known him or her.

When reversed: Make sure you're speaking clearly; high-strung emotions could cloud your message. You have very little patience just now. Try to relax. Let go of all your worries.

VIII OF CUPS

Self-sacrifice is likely to be asked of you. Beware of quarrels; use caution in negoti-ating affairs of the heart. Attention spans are running short, so don't take anything too personally. Count your blessings and try to be content with what you have.

When reversed: Emotions run high. Let go of situations that no longer concern you. Spend some time and money on the things that make you feel good.

IX OF CUPS

People are generous to those in need. Enjoy the kindness of strangers. Stay away from shop-talk and try not to worry about finances.

When reversed: Postpone decision-making. Weigh your options. No one minces words now. Beware of arrogance—try to be easy going.

X OF CUPS

 Tender words and sympathy bring the best results. Speak from your heart. A sudden flirtation or love affair is likely. Food and drink become more appealing now, so try not to overdo it. Leave the answering machine on and let someone else answer the door.

When reversed: Be kind to strangers, as well as to yourself. Your emotions are unfocused. Be discreet. Follow through on promises made.

THE SUIT OF PENTACLES

Also known as Coins, Pentacle cards represent money matters. They speak of work, career, and everything material, real, and solid. When they fall upright, Pentacles tell you that you're in control. When reversed, they suggest confusion about material concerns and susceptibility to intimidation from those who hold power over you.

PAGE OF PENTACLES

 You want to be financially independent, so why not get started right away? You may have to put up with criticism from family and friends, but this is the time to push forward and improve your quality of life!

When reversed: You're being hesitant, secretly doubting that you'll succeed. Do not be afraid of a little competition.

KNIGHT OF PENTACLES

 You've been questioning whether you'll ever have enough money to get the things you want and need. You rarely feel discouraged, but lately you lack confidence in the future. Success is around the corner, but first you must learn to budget time and money better.

When reversed: The key to your future financial security is to stop overspending. Cut back. Start looking at bottom lines, what you owe, and to whom you owe it.

QUEEN OF PENTACLES

You may be doubting your ability to live up to your responsibilities. Believe in yourself, but don't look for too much approval from others at this time. Rewards will arrive when you work independently, in your own way.

When reversed: What you lack in daring, you make up for in perseverance. Stay focused; don't let others scatter your energies or sway you off course.

KING OF PENTACLES

Stop trying to be a jack-of-all-trades. Specialize. You have strong sensual and physical desires just now. Don't let your sense of self-discipline interfere with your personal happiness and fulfillment.

When reversed: You're being extremely sensitive now, more vulnerable to the suggestions of others. Stop it! Fear of competition and growth will only delay desired outcomes. Act now to meet your goals. Tell your partners your objectives and feelings. Don't be afraid of rejection.

ACE OF PENTACLES

This card heralds good luck with new business acknowledgment and endeavors for a job well done. This is a great time to apply for new work or seek a promotion. Enjoy—and demand—life's pleasures.

When reversed: Don't let self-doubt get the best of you. Money may become tight. Beware of reckless, irresponsible people. Surround yourself with colleagues looking out for your best interests.

II OF PENTACLES

Let go of something old in preparation for new opportunities. Keep your ears tuned to alternative business proposals. Brainstorm with peers, explore teamwork.

When reversed: Reflect carefully about your motives before dealing with people. Act with integrity and you'll be sure to find success in all your endeavors.

III OF PENTACLES

Achievement in business is at hand, chiefly because you're willing to make yourself available to your supervisors. But be careful not to buy others with gifts—this will only lead to resentment.

When reversed: Don't let your insecurity drive you to be overly generous to the needy—you'll end up with less energy and less money.

IV OF PENTACLES

Manage your money with firm ethics. Respect those in power but do not accept intimidation. Your ideas are rich but still need development.

When reversed: The demands of personal security weigh heavily on you now. Confusion and loss are likely if you let greed or insecurity take over. Challenge and opposition are on the horizon. Meet them head on.

V OF PENTACLES

Your hard work and devotion to others may not be paying off. Let others know what you expect in return. Temporary health and financial problems may be ahead.

When reversed: Learn the virtues of self-discipline and teamwork—these will bring rewards. Others try to make you conform. Reserve the right to express yourself as you choose. Repaid loans or a new source of income are likely.

VI OF PENTACLES

 You will soon profit from the extra efforts you've been putting forth. Stop being overly sensitive to the needs of others at work. Beware of overindulgence.

When reversed: Don't let your insecurities push you into being a workaholic. Choose well-defined objectives that will bring growth. Slow down. Try not to borrow money now—new obligations will take the starch out of your sails.

VII OF PENTACLES

Have you been jumping the gun lately? Patience and hard work bring success. Try to listen to others and postpone decisions until you're informed. You hate to be broke, but don't over-burden yourself to make ends meet.

When reversed: You may like to have the final word, but there's no harm in asking for advice. Take your time to make informed decisions.

VIII OF PENTACLES

You want what's best for your loved ones and coworkers, and you have the strength to provide it. But you have lots to learn. If you lack information, have the determination to find it!

When reversed: You'll soon gain recognition for accomplishments. Don't forget those who made your success possible. You want to help people, so be a willing listener.

IX OF PENTACLES

Look for opportunities to develop your creative potential and to prove what you can do. Start now! The time for paybacks and rewards is quickly approaching, but it will only come if you strive for success.

When reversed: Plan carefully for whatever you hope to achieve right now. Don't assume everything will work out just as expected, and don't be afraid to ask for help.

X OF PENTACLES

Your imagination is second to none, so express yourself. Your talents are in demand. Just as you attain one goal, another will emerge. Be prudent and confident. Make plans and refuse to be deterred from your new objective.

When reversed: You've been busy helping others. Keep your own goals foremost in your mind. Friends will show their true colors. Be on the lookout for legal entanglements.

THE SUIT OF SWORDS

Swords relate to intellectual pursuits, social interactions, and aggression. They can cut two ways. Sometimes they represent breakthroughs in communication; other times, breakdowns. When the cards fall in upright positions, you're likely to be victorious. When they fall reversed, they indicate confusion and a need to look at things more objectively.

PAGE OF SWORDS

 Do you resent the intrusions of others in your life? Make a break. Assert yourself. Those who truly love you will continue to stand by you.

When reversed: You often change your course of action as you work toward your goals. This isn't necessarily bad, as long as you keep your goals clearly in focus. Friends may make excessive demands. Decline kindly but firmly.

KNIGHT OF SWORDS

You're an understanding listener and you know just what to say to please others. But don't get so close to associates that you have a hard time thinking for yourself. Rely on your own ability to solve problems.

When reversed: Troublemakers surround you. Deal with them openly and boldly to keep them from dominating your thinking and blocking your talents.

QUEEN OF SWORDS

Let others suffer the consequences of their actions. Be your own person and you won't get burned.

When reversed: Heavy demands make you feel doubt. Loyalty is admirable, but don't dwell too much on the past. You have a mind of your own—assert it! You don't need anyone else's approval.

KING OF SWORDS

 Your keen imagination helps you achieve independence. Cultivate your talents. Seek the company of those who truly care about you.

When reversed: Jealousy abounds—in you or those around you. Watch out for narrow minds and prejudice. Develop your intellectual skills; play your hunches.

ACE OF SWORDS

Your spirit is strong and pioneering. Don't let your ego get in the way. This is a good time to push ahead with ideas, contract negotiations, and other legal matters. Goals you can meet quickly are better than long-range ones.

When reversed: Things are out of balance. Practice patience and perseverance. This is the time for some solo work. In your dealings with others, don't distort the facts.

II OF SWORDS

Tensions begin to mellow. Help is on the way. Slow down and relax—you're entering a leisurely phase. Make yourself available to others, but don't spread yourself too thin.

When reversed: Your ability to see merit in all arguments hampers your ability to make decisions. Don't vacillate. Aim for cooperation, not confrontation.

III OF SWORDS

You misinterpret another's intentions. This could be a time of regret or separation, so keep your chin up and look for the light at the end of the tunnel. Don't let nerv-ousness or worry cloud clear thinking and action.

When reversed: Progress is sluggish; delays are inevitable. Are you looking at things honestly? Find ways to take control of the situation.

IV OF SWORDS

To soothe disagreements, look for a conservative, middle-of-the-road position. The opposition lessens when you realize that people can change. The greatest obstacle to your success is impatience.

When reversed: You're likely to experience difficulties in communicating with others. Let associates lend a hand. Don't get bogged down by the past. Family, friends, and coworkers bring answers soon.

V OF SWORDS

You're feeling overwhelmed and low in spirits. Now is the time for reprioritizing. You are not as powerless as you may feel.

When reversed: Beware of pessimism and low self-esteem. You'll have to work harder, and success may not come quickly, but things will soon begin to turn around. Don't neglect your health and diet. Allow yourself some time for play.

VI OF SWORDS

To achieve security and happiness you've got to plan your goals carefully now. Knowing when to say no will help you maintain your integrity. Take some time for yourself.

When reversed: Your greatest accomplishments come through competition. Learn from the opposition. Look outside yourself for alternative courses of action. Solutions become clear when you get away from day-to-day duties.

VII OF SWORDS

 Making plans becomes problematic. Friends may let you down. Don't rely too much on others. You can't lose what's not yours to begin with. Get everything in writing.

When reversed: Pressures are on the rise. Don't take on too much. Learn from the successes and failures of others.

VIII OF SWORDS

 Gossip is in the air. Be easy-going when you encounter opposition from stubborn people. Postpone ultimatums. Don't accept everything as a fact. Update your résumé and open your mind to new business deals. Think about current and future financial needs.

When reversed: This is a slowing-down period that delivers options and freedom from restrictions. Results won't be instant.

IX OF SWORDS

Depression, suspicion, and self-doubt cloud your sense of purpose. Don't lose your focus.

When reversed: Confusion and poor decision-making are in the air. Your step falters and progress is delayed. A good time for second thoughts.

X OF SWORDS

 Trouble in personal relationships has been weighing on your mind. Your ability to solve problems can be determined only when you apply what you know and feel.

When reversed: Someone you love or respect will soon give you the stimulus you need to put your talents to good use. If you can resolve your self-doubts and fears, you'll soon prove your abilities.

THE SUIT OF WANDS

The realm of Wands is that of physical energy, growth, and personal enterprise. When the cards fall upright in a layout, you're in the driver's seat. When reversed, someone else is at the steering wheel.

PAGE OF WANDS

 Tact and diplomacy will bring the best results. People are in a generous mood, so don't hesitate to ask for assistance and get matters off your chest.

When reversed: Everyone wants to get things done quickly. Don't overlook important details in the rush to completion.

KNIGHT OF WANDS

 The more self-assured you are, the better things will go. Everybody's playing to win, so be prepared for competition. Fight the need to have the final word.

When reversed: Don't believe everything you hear. Beware of impatience and the white lies of others. Stand firm in your convictions, but know when to swallow your pride.

QUEEN OF WANDS

Believe in yourself—don't be afraid to take the lead. Dealings with authority figures go well. Answers arrive when you talk things out with friends and lovers. Write letters, make calls, send faxes. Punctuality really counts.

When reversed: Bet only what you can afford to lose; don't take silly risks. Guard against unrealistic thinking. Dare to dream, but keep both feet firmly on the ground.

KING OF WANDS

You're about to be surprisingly successful in navigating extremely complex situations as you strive to meet some of your long-range goals. Use your intuition and treat others royally. Cooperation in professional projects brings great rewards.

When reversed: Seek new options for growth and mobilize your skills. Stay firmly within ethical boundaries when you act, and don't be too aggressive.

ACE OF WANDS

Now is the time for sending out résumés, starting a new enterprise, or beginning a journey. Your strength uplifts those who lack the resources to solve their problems alone.

When reversed: It pains you when you don't have the answers to the questions others ask. Remain strong.

II OF WANDS

Be a willing listener. Knowing what people need gives you an advantage. Help is on the way, even though you have the self-confidence to succeed on your own. Reexamine your goals and define exactly what it is that you want to achieve.

When reversed: Don't rely too much on loved ones or business associates for advice. Trust your own instincts to get you through a crisis.

III OF WANDS

You are very good at putting the talents and skills of others to their best use. Be specific about what you want and don't be misled by well-meaning friends. This is not a lonely time. Use the strength of those around you—teamwork brings luck.

When reversed: Stop struggling! Stay focused and don't be intimidated by know-it-alls. Ask questions. Take time to define what you want clearly.

IV OF WANDS

Social life and activity come to the forefront. Don't get stuck in old behavior patterns. If you come to a fork in the road, keep your eyes open for all options. Past efforts and labor bring rewards.

When reversed: Try to appreciate what you have; don't let envy into your life. Errors in judgment are likely when emotions cloud reason. Do you really think someone is taking advantage of you? Think about it.

V OF WANDS

People around you are cranky; morale is low. Stay calm through the chaos, and remember who you are. Read all of the fine print—legal troubles are possible now.

When reversed: You don't always have to come out on top. Accept compromises and apologies. Reprioritize.

VI OF WANDS

Competition brings out the best in you. Don't be afraid to ask some questions. Apologies are in the stars.

When reversed: Everyone—including you—wants to have things his or her way now. Sit it out, bide your time.

VII OF WANDS

 Faith overcomes your current obstacles. You have the power to accomplish your goals. Consider all of the consequences, but act swiftly.

When reversed: Don't be indecisive. Say what you feel and move on. Situations are nowhere near resolution, so be patient.

VIII OF WANDS

All your plans have a green light. Move ahead. Your understanding of people and their problems delivers opportunities to get what you want. Friends and nature bring remedies for what ails you.

When reversed: Your energy is scattered. Think before you act. Don't ignore the chain of command.

IX OF WANDS

 Fight for and hold onto what you believe. Your projects are near completion; relaxation is at hand. Victory soon arrives. Luck comes to children.

When reversed: Be prepared and aware of the ruler of the game. Arrogance creates obstacles. Rid yourself of self-pity and anxiety. Tend to your health.

X OF WANDS

The aggressive pursuit of your goals will result in serious setbacks with superiors until you learn to be more restrained and original. Break out of stubborn patterns and look for new approaches. An on-the-job transfer or change of status is likely.

When reversed: Focus your energy or you'll waste it. Be sure you have an objective in mind, and you're not just blowing off steam.

HOW TO CONDUCT A READING

THE TAROT, LIKE THE I CHING or ancient rune stones, provides tips and clues about your life—not answers. The cards provoke introspection. They urge you to think about your goals and motives and to take a look at how you interact with the world.

You can conduct a reading for yourself or for somebody else. If you're reading the cards for a friend, have your friend perform the first two steps that follow. If you're reading your own cards, perform all steps yourself.

1 · Hold the deck of cards face down and shuffle through them for about fifteen seconds. Don't think of anything in particular. Keep your mind clear. Focus on the shuffling and nothing else. (Or, if you prefer, you can concentrate on a primary concern or question. But if you keep your mind clear, the Tarot will suggest an issue for you.)

2 · Using your left hand, cut the deck into four piles, moving from left to right as shown below.

3 · Take the top card from the far-left pile and turn it face up on the table in front of you. (Place it in position **A** on the chart to the right.) This indicates what part of your life the reading will address. It may refer to a situation that is currently causing you concern, a problem you're trying to resolve or will soon face, an area of your life you need to work on improving, or one that will soon bring you great joy. Consider this card an outsider's view, an objective observation.

A
What's
at Hand

B
Past
Influences

C
Ponder
This

D
What
to Do

4 • Take the top card from your second pile and turn it face up beneath and to the left of card **A**. (Place it in position **B** on the chart.) This card suggests past events, situations, and relationships that might be influencing the situation represented by card **A**.

5 • Place the top card from your third pile face up in position **C**. This card offers food for thought, things to ponder in light of card **A**.

6 • Finally, turn the top card of your fourth pile face up in position **D**. This card suggests answers or courses of action.

The pages of this journal include interpretations of the seventy-eight cards in the Tarot. Refer to these descriptions to help you understand the meaning of your layout. Always bear in mind what each card's position represents. And don't limit yourself to the interpretations provided here—if the art on the cards inspires other ideas, use them. In addition, here are a few general tips.

• Cards will either fall upright or reversed. When a card is *reversed*, either its meaning is not as strong, its meaning is more extreme, or an external influence has more power than you over the situation. A majority of reversed cards in a layout warns against laziness and depending too much on others. A majority of *upright* cards says you're in control—it's a good time to take action.

UPRIGHT   **REVERSED**

• Note which group of cards is dominant in a reading. Several **Major Arcana** cards signal that you should take matters more seriously. A majority of **Cups** warns against letting your feelings cloud reason. Lots of **Swords** forewarn indecision on your part. **Wands** say you should act while you're exuberant and full of energy. **Pentacles** tell you to approach everything like an accountant and aim for profit. The layout shown here is a basic layout that can be used with any deck.

• There are many layouts you can use, and you shouldn't hesitate to design your own. As long as you develop a consistent rationale and assign specific meanings and values to each position in the layout, the Tarot will conform to your customized design. Have fun!